After the Snowflakes

Written by
Kitty Kaye

Illustrated by
Debbe Femiak

To my own little snowflakes -
Malachi, Mason & Micah.
They are each as unique and special
as they come.

After the snowflakes come...

...I can slide down the hill on my new toboggan.

After the snowflakes come...

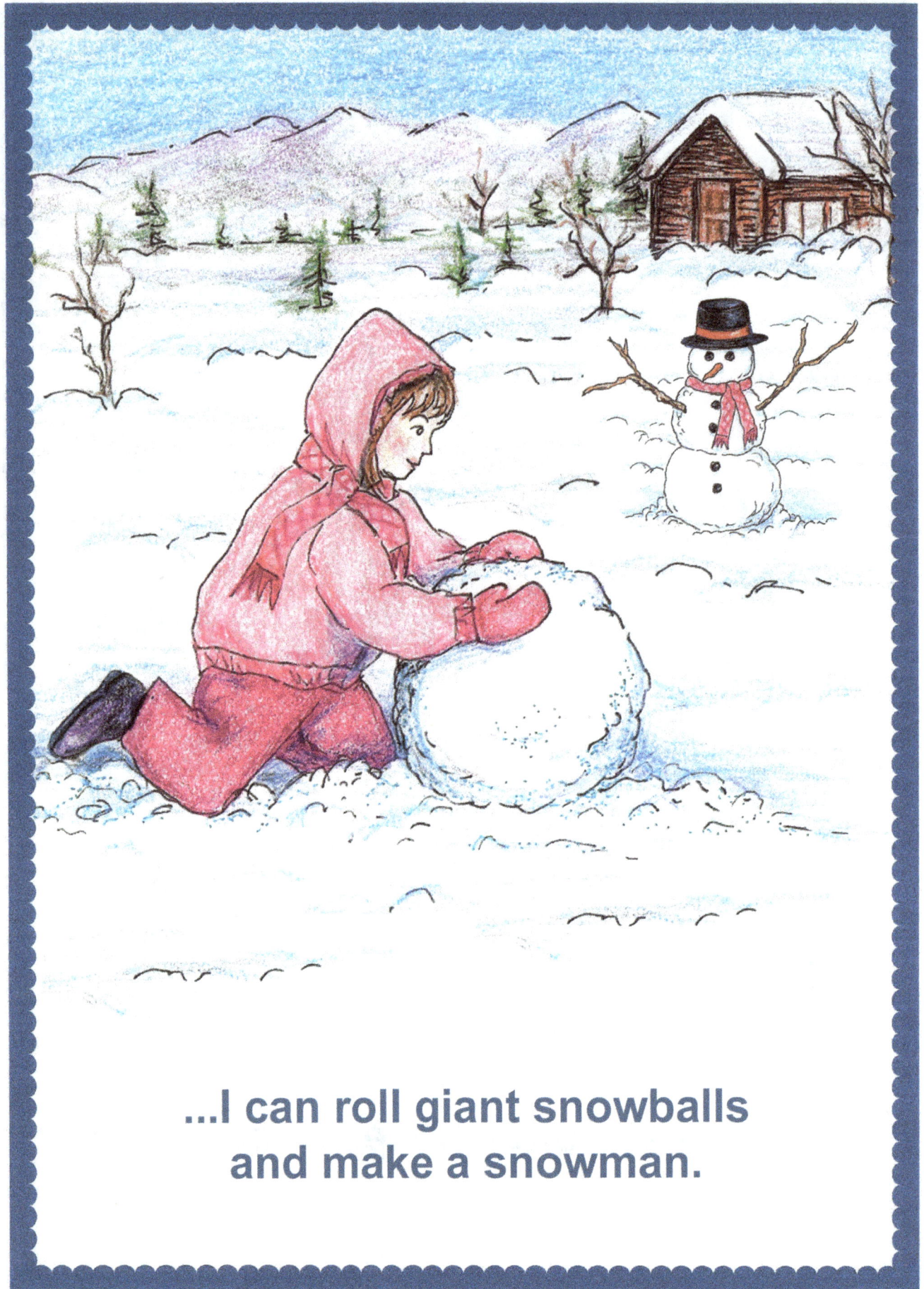

...I can roll giant snowballs
and make a snowman.

After the snowflakes come...

...I can ski as fast as the wind...

...or snowshoe quietly through the forest.

Sometimes I like to just catch the
snowflakes on my tongue...

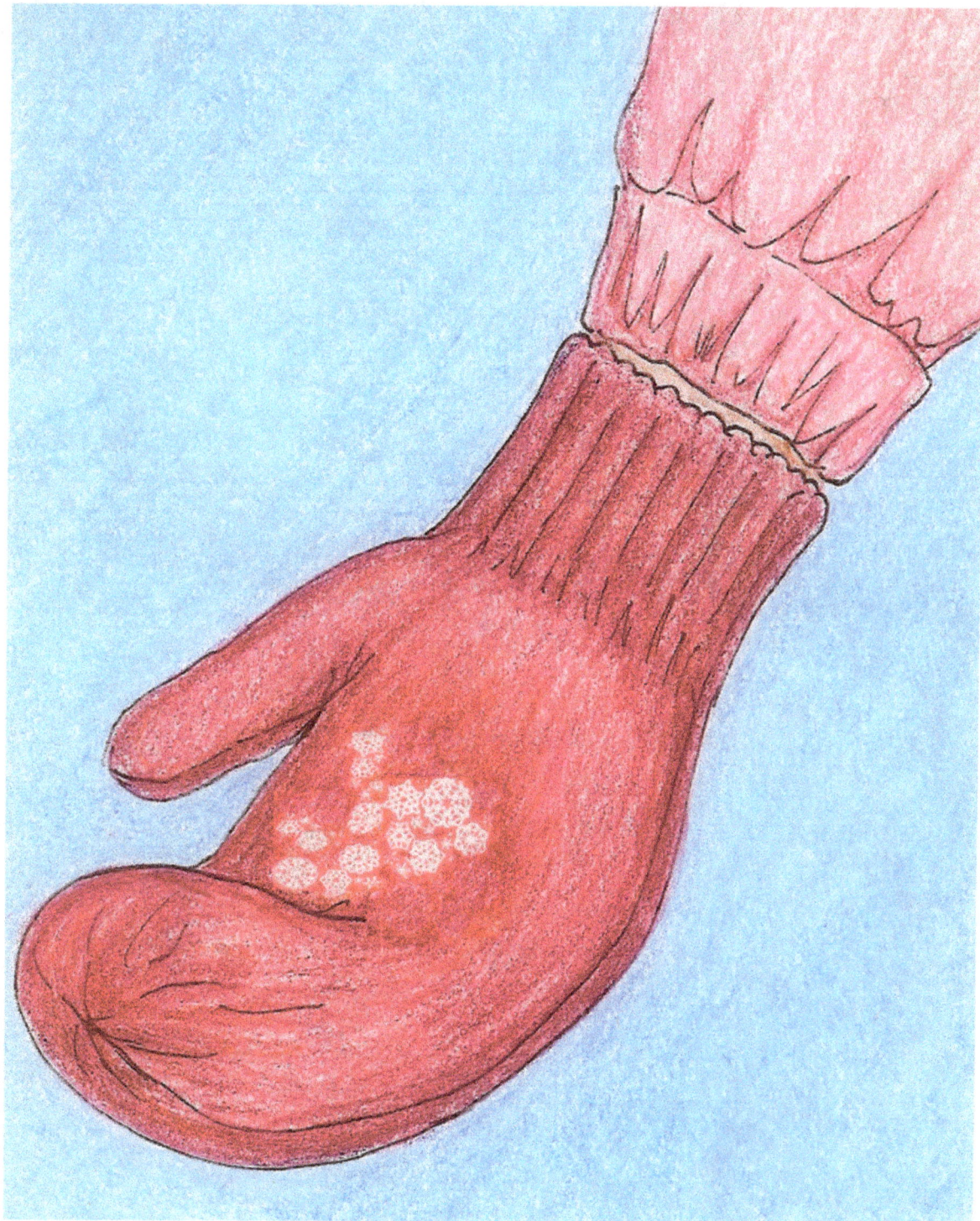

...watch them melt on my mitten...

...or make my own special snow angel.

Someday soon the sun will get warmer, and the snowflakes will start to melt...

...but I'm going to enjoy them
as long as I can.

Aren't they beautiful?!

Snowflakes

*Snowflakes are an
amazing thing,
they make me want
to dance and sing.*

*They swirl and twirl
'round and 'round,
as they drift down
to the ground.*

*Each so different,
no two the same,
as they glide through the air
in a magical game.*

*Snowflakes come on a
cold winter's day,
and invite us all
to come out and play.*

Kitty Kaye

OTHER CHILDREN'S BOOKS BY THE AUTHOR

Sunny Boy

Written by Kitty Kaye
Illustrated by
Christopher McCue and Michelle Wright

Sunny is the brightest star in the universe, but struggles to find his place in life. By forming a true friendship, Sunny finds he is able to become successful. **Sunny Boy** is an illustrated children's book that has a good message for any reader.

Grandma Kitty's *Coloring Book* of Poetry

Written by Kitty Kaye

Illustrated by Debbe Femiak

Grandma Kitty's Coloring Book of Poetry is a book for coloring, filled with encouraging poetry verses. The children's verses are to help build self-esteem and promote acceptable behaviors. The adult verses are for those who have faced challenging situations. Each page has an illustration to color and is suitable for framing upon completion.

ISBN: 978-1-7331639-4-1

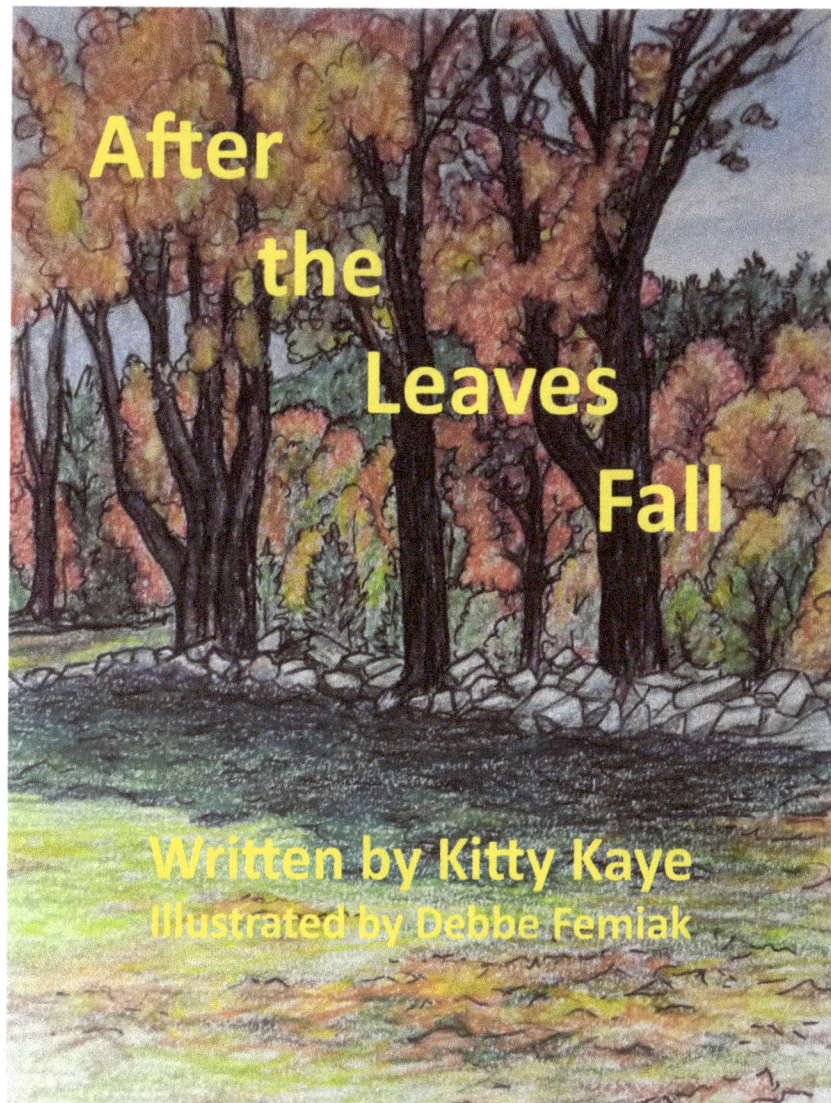

Each beautifully illustrated page of **After the Leaves Fall** shows fun ways to celebrate the season of autumn. Also included are pages showing the different shapes and colors of leaves. The book ends with a poem about autumn leaves, encouraging the reader to enjoy the colorful season of fall.